Tudor
Age of
Discovery

This is a story about exploration, discovery and settlement. It is one of those rare times when whole new parts of the world were explored.

In some ways, you can think of the lands the Tudors and others reached in the 1500s as the 'Wild West' of Tudor times. There were three kinds of people on the journey: those who simply wanted adventure; those who wanted money; and those whose lives were difficult at home and so they wanted a new start. However, the land they came to was not empty, but occupied by nations with their own culture. This is the story of those explorers.

Dr Brian Knapp

Curriculum Visions

There's much more on-line including videos

You will find multimedia resources covering more Tudor topics and many more history, science, geography, religion and spelling subjects in the Professional Zone at:

www.CurriculumVisions.com

A CVP Book
Copyright © 2007 Earthscape

Author
Brian Knapp, BSc, PhD

Researcher
Lisa Magloff, MA

Senior Designer
Adele Humphries, BA, PGCE

Editors
Jan Smith (former Deputy Head of Wellfield School, Burnley, Lancashire) and Gillian Gatehouse

Designed and produced by
EARTHSCAPE

Printed in China by
WKT Company Ltd

Tudor Age of Discovery – *Curriculum Visions*
A CIP record for this book is available from the British Library

Paperback ISBN: 978 1 86214 240 4
Hardback ISBN: 978 1 86214 241 1

Illustrations
David Woodroffe pages 2–3, 6–7, 8–9, 14–15, 40;
Mark Stacey page 36.

Picture credits
All photographs are from the Earthscape Picture Library except the following: (c=centre t=top b=bottom l=left r=right) *Alamy* pages 41, 43tr; *Corbis* page 29; *The Granger Collection, New York* pages 26–27 (main), 35; *ShutterStock* pages 1, 7, 8–9, 11tr, 12tr, 17br, 18bc, 22–23, 26 (Drake and Elizabeth I), 32–33, 44–45; *TopFoto* pages 5, 10–11 (main), 12–13 (main), 16–17 (main), 18–19 (main), 20, 21, 25, 30–31, 32 (Raleigh), 34, 37, 38–39, 42, 43 (main).

This product is manufactured from sustainable managed forests. For every tree cut down at least one more is planted.

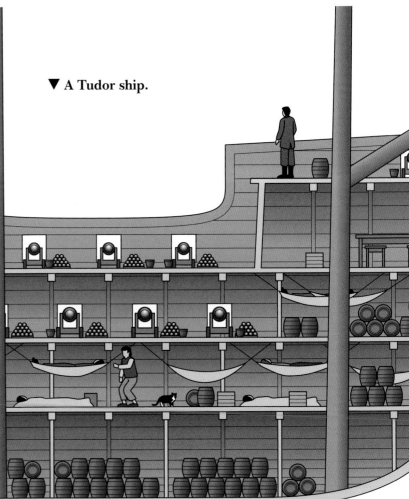

▼ A Tudor ship.

Contents

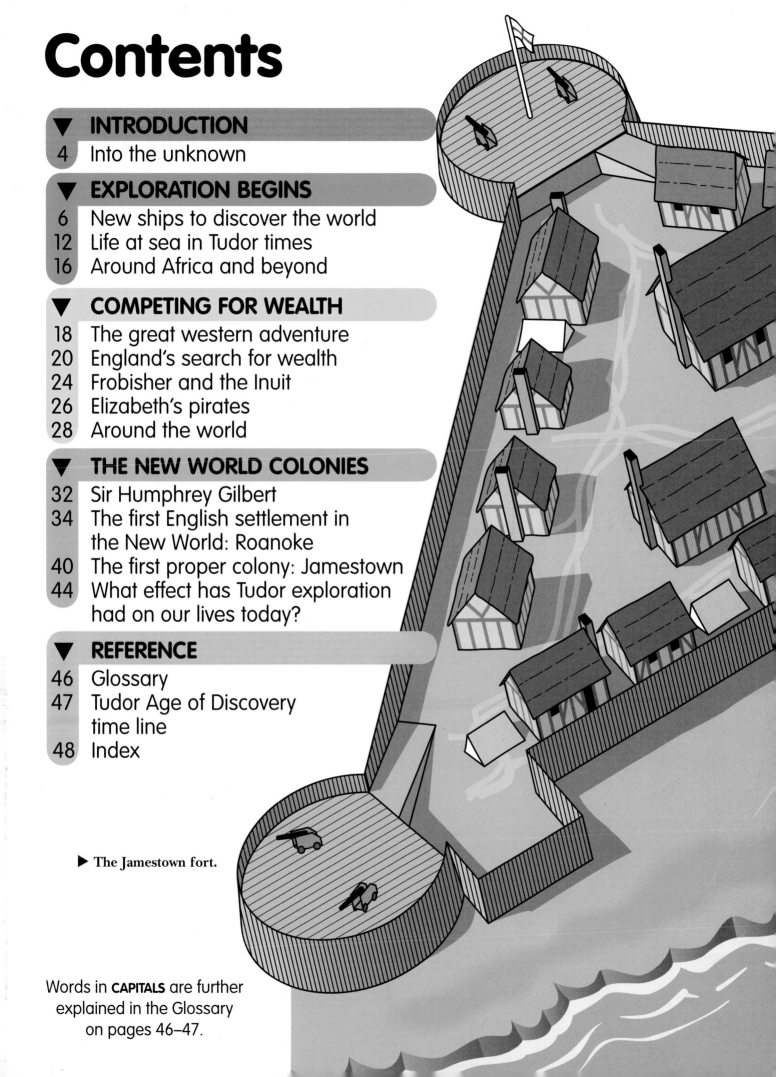

▼ **INTRODUCTION**

4 Into the unknown

▼ **EXPLORATION BEGINS**

6 New ships to discover the world
12 Life at sea in Tudor times
16 Around Africa and beyond

▼ **COMPETING FOR WEALTH**

18 The great western adventure
20 England's search for wealth
24 Frobisher and the Inuit
26 Elizabeth's pirates
28 Around the world

▼ **THE NEW WORLD COLONIES**

32 Sir Humphrey Gilbert
34 The first English settlement in the New World: Roanoke
40 The first proper colony: Jamestown
44 What effect has Tudor exploration had on our lives today?

▼ **REFERENCE**

46 Glossary
47 Tudor Age of Discovery time line
48 Index

▶ The Jamestown fort.

Words in **CAPITALS** are further explained in the Glossary on pages 46–47.

Into the unknown

No one knew what lay to the west and most were too frightened to find out.

By the 1400s, Europe was more peaceful than it had been for hundreds of years. Without the cost of war, it was a time when MERCHANTS and kings were getting richer – and they wanted to become richer still.

The unknown west

If you stood at Lands End on the southwestern tip of England at this time and looked south, you would have been looking towards two of the world's most powerful countries: Spain and France. The centre of the world was Jerusalem, far off to the south east and known to you from pilgrimages and the CRUSADES, but if you had turned and looked to the west, then you would have had no idea what lay beyond the horizon.

The great ocean to the west – the Atlantic Ocean – went on, some said, until the end of the world was reached. Then, if you sailed further, you simply fell off the edge.

A closed world

You can see how much the Europeans knew of the world by looking at the map opposite (picture ①). You will see other maps as you go through the book, and it will always be useful to compare them to this one.

At this time, Europeans thought that Europe, Asia and (North) Africa was surrounded by one vast ocean.

In search of wealth

The Greeks had been the first people to show that the Earth was round and by the 1400s many people took this for granted. But most still feared the open ocean. Tales of great sea monsters still worried sailors in their little wooden boats.

No-one had struck out across the open ocean because their boats were too small and not strong enough to battle storm waves.

In any case, Europeans were not really interested in the west at all. They were interested in gold and silver, spices and slaves. These came from Asia and Africa in the east.

Then a curious series of events occurred which resulted in the Europeans discovering many new places. That is why it came to be called the AGE OF DISCOVERY. That is what we shall be looking at in this book.

However, to see how this all came about we shall need to go back several centuries, to the time of the famous traveller Marco Polo.

◀ The Mappa Mundi has east at the top, like this. Modern maps have north at the top.

▼ ① The Mappa Mundi is a map of the known world before the Age of Discovery. At that time the centre of the known world was thought of as Jerusalem. The top of this map is east and the bottom is west. The long sea with islands in is the Mediterranean. Europe, Asia and North Africa were all known. The New World (the Americas), Australia and the Antarctic were unknown to them.

E

Jerusalem

N

S

British Isles

W

New ships to discover the world

Traditional ships were not able to stand up to the fierce Atlantic waves. But then new ship design and competition between European countries made all the difference.

Why had no one ventured far from Europe before? The ships were not good enough to cope with fierce ocean storms, and navigation was poor, so that, if you left sight of land there was only a slim chance you would find your way home. During the age of the Viking explorers (800–1100 AD), for example, many Viking ships had been lost for this reason (picture ①).

Ships were also too small. All they could do was to carry the men who manned them. They were not very good at carrying cargo or even food and water for the sailors.

However, after Viking times, people began to design new styles of ship. They were a cross between the Viking longship and Arabs DHOW (which had triangular sails). They were used for fishing (picture ②). From this, shipbuilders in Portugal developed a completely new form of merchant ship. It was called a **CARRACK**, meaning 'barge' (pictures ③ and ④). (The warship versions later became known as galleons – picture ⑦ pages 8–9.) But this was no ordinary barge. It was the supertanker of its day.

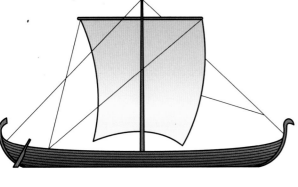

▲ ① Until the Middle Ages, ships had a single central mast, like this Viking longship.

▶ ② In the Middle Ages, fishing boats were developed with multiple sails. This is where the carrack and caravel designs came from.

▶ ③ A reconstructed carrack – Christopher Columbus' Santa Maria – in full sail.

The carrack

The carrack was designed to carry cargo for merchants. It had many advantages:

- Carracks could carry enough food and water so they didn't have to keep putting in to port (and so having to stay near the coast).

- Their sides were tall enough so that small ships in foreign parts could not attack them.

- They had high **FORECASTLES** and **STERNCASTLES** for soldiers to shoot at enemies.

- They had several sails: the big one(s) in the middle for pushing the boat forwards, the smaller ones fore and aft to help with stability and to steer across the wind.

- They had flat decks on which cannon could be mounted.

▶ ④ The carrack was a large ship, which sat high in the water and had tall forecastles and sterncastles. It had a single large sail in the middle of the ship.

Weblink: www.CurriculumVisions.com

The caravel

Carracks were not as manoeuvrable as captains wanted for exploration into shallow coastal waters or up river estuaries. As a result, smaller versions of the design were built, often of about 50 to 100 tons and 20–30 m long, sleeker in plan and without the high forecastles and sterncastles. These were called **CARAVELS** (pictures ⑤ and ⑥).

Now explorers could have a 'mother ship' – the carrack – supported by smaller caravels. Everything was set for discovery. When Christopher Columbus set out on his famous expedition to China and found the 'New World' in 1492 he had a carrack – the Santa Maria – as his flagship (mother ship) and he was accompanied by the smaller caravels Pinta and Niña. Most Tudor age explorers did much the same.

▼ ⑤ The reconstructed carrack – the Santa Maria – of Christopher Columbus (centre) plus her two caravels – the Pinta and Niña.

▼ ⑥ The caravel was a smaller version of the carrack and had no forecastles or sterncastles.

▶ ⑦ The galleon was a large carrack designed for fighting battles. (The Ark Royal was a galleon commissioned by Henry VIII.) It had no forecastle and more sail near the bow of the ship. It had multiple sails on its masts. Similar designs became the merchant ships of the 17th century, bringing trade from the East Indies.

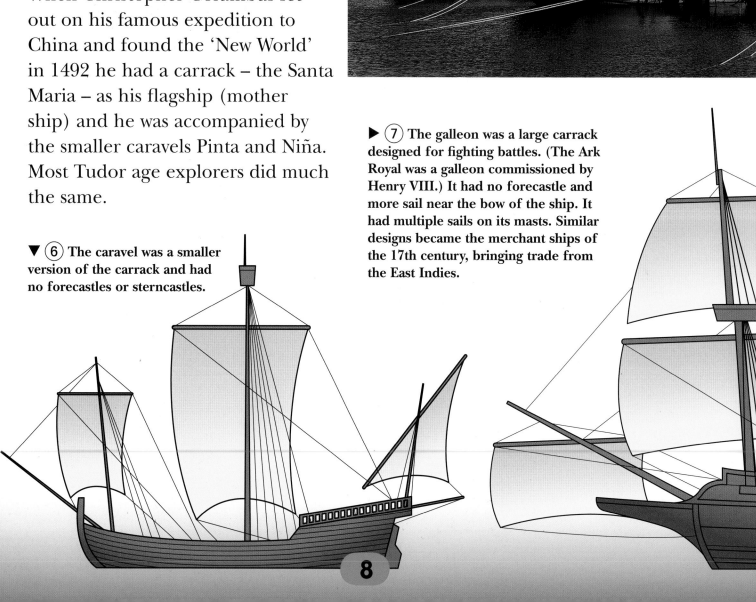

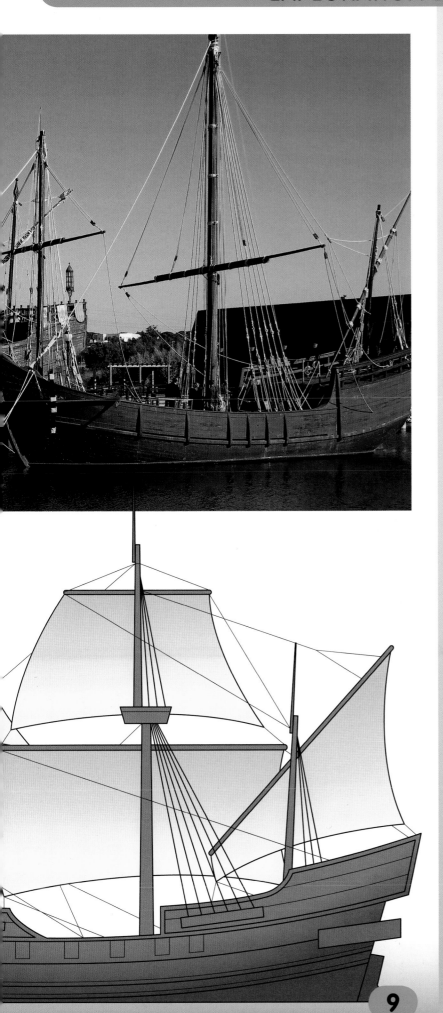

The Golden Hind

The Golden Hind, the carrack used by Sir Francis Drake on his voyage around the world (see pages 28–31), was typical of the ships used during the Age of Discovery (see pictures on pages 10–11). It was a cargo ship and also a **MAN O'WAR**. It had 18 guns, it was 21 metres long and weighed about 100 tonnes. It had 20 officers, 60 crew and three boys to act as lookouts from the crow's nests at the top of the masts.

All such ships needed **BALLAST** to stop them toppling over. On the way out this was made of boulders. It was hoped that, on the way back, the rocks could be replaced with treasure!

The ship had three masts. The two middle masts were used to catch the full force of the wind and so push the ship forwards. There was also a **BOWSPRIT** to keep the ship stable in the water.

Drake's cabin was the only room with a bed. The other officers slept in the armoury on straw mattresses.

Crow's nest

The crow's nest was the place the boys sat. They would get the first sight of land (or an enemy vessel).

The great cabin

Below Drake's cabin was the great cabin where Drake entertained the officers and also the captains and officers from other ships (such as the Spanish ships he raided).

Mast

The mast was made from one piece of wood, but if it broke disaster faced the crew, so ships carried spares.

Drake's cabin

Drake's cabin had its own bed.

▼ Spices such as nutmeg and cloves, together with gold and silver, were the treasure the ships sought.

Cinnamon

Star Anise

Nutmeg

Cardamon

Cloves

▲ Flush boarding essential for making the ship watertight.

▼ The Golden Hind was painted on the stern. You can also see the Tudor rose and the letters ER (for Elizabeth Regina).

CASSIS TVTIS SIMA VIRTVS

Life at sea in Tudor times

Sea journeys were very dangerous and less than half the crew would usually survive a long journey. There were the risks of poor weather, starvation or thirst, disease, warfare and accidents. So why go at all?

Life on land in the 16th century was very hard, and life expectancy was very low. Going to sea was a great adventure where the pay could be relatively good.

Signing on with a privateer like Sir Francis Drake (see page 27) made it possible for a sailor to win glory and fame, and capture fabulous wealth. The crew usually received a small portion of whatever booty was captured. But in any case, they could bring back small amounts of trade goods – selling even

▶ ① **Nutmeg.**

a small bag of nutmeg in England would be enough to make a man rich for life (picture ①).

Navigation

Ocean voyages were very dangerous because ships were small, there were no accurate maps and no accurate way to navigate long distances.

There were several ways to find the latitude (how far north or south you are from the Equator) while at sea, but longitude (how far east or west you are) could be little more than a calculated guess, which they called dead reckoning.

To estimate the position of his ship a Tudor navigator had to determine:

- The direction his ship was travelling in.
- How long the ship had travelled in this direction.
- The speed of the ship.

The Tudor seafarer plotted his direction from his home port on a chart and tried to steer his ship in this direction guided by a magnetic compass.

Because there were no accurate clocks, sailors measured the length of time the ship travelled along this course using a sand-glass timer, which had to be turned over regularly and was not very accurate.

The speed of a ship was calculated by throwing a log attached to a knotted piece of rope overboard. This was known as the ship's log. As the ship moved away from the log the sailor counted how many knots were let out behind the ship in a fixed period of time. This method was not very accurate because it did not take into account the winds and currents.

The Tudors used instruments called the quadrant and the astrolabe (picture ②) to measure the height of the Sun or the Pole Star above the horizon.

▼ ② A sailor using the astrolabe, 1583.

Knowing this value and the starting point of the journey allowed the navigator to work out the latitude, and from that make an educated guess about the ship's position.

Bedding

Only the captain had a room to himself. Crew slept on deck in the hot latitudes, and below in colder areas. Sailors slept in hammocks or on the floor (picture ③). Half the crew would sleep while the other half was on duty. Sailors didn't have much space on board. They would have only been allowed a small chest to keep their belongings in.

Toilets

Near the bow of the ship there was a small hole, which served as the crew's toilet. The officers, including the captain, used holes in the sterncastle or a bucket.

Food

The hold was where the stores were kept. Stores included water, salted meat, beans and hard biscuits. There were often maggots in the biscuits, which were either eaten or picked out, depending on

how fussy the sailor was (maggots were, after all, a good source of protein!).

Barrels of water were kept below, but the water often went bad before it ran out. When the water went bad, the sailors turned to weak beer. Beer is alcoholic and alcohol helps to preserve the beer so that it stays fresh for longer than the water.

The ships had live animals on board to provide fresh meat and eggs, but this was usually reserved for the officers.

Before leaving land, meat was salted and kept in barrels, but this soon rotted.

When the Tudor sailors did eat meat, it would have to be cooked. This was done on a brazier, a box of sand with a fire on it over which food could be cooked and water boiled. The sand box was crucial: the whole ship was made of wood, so fire was very risky and could only be used in calm weather. The sand protected the ship from the flames.

Sickness

Sailors were often sick during their voyages. The most common complaint was scurvy, an illness brought on because sailors were not getting enough fresh fruit and vegetables. At first, scurvy made sailors' gums bleed, finally, all their teeth would fall out. Scurvy was very painful and if left untreated sailors would often die from the disease. It was not unusual for over half the crew to die of scurvy or other diseases on a long voyage.

Ships were usually infested with rats. Traditionally every ship carried at least one cat on board to kill rats. Sailors thought that black and white cats were the luckiest cats to have on board.

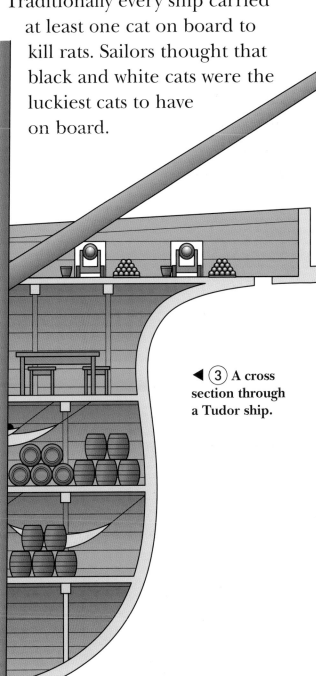

◀ ③ A cross section through a Tudor ship.

Around Africa and beyond

There had been conflict between Muslims and Christians for centuries. With the Turks occupying North Africa and the Middle East, supplies of gold and silver were running out.

In the thirteenth century (300 years before the Age of Discovery) two brothers from the powerful city of Venice, Niccolo and Maffeo Polo, made a journey to China by land. In 1292, the Polos returned to Europe with detailed maps and instructions for the trade route to Asia, as well as giving details of the goods that could be traded along the way.

Land routes are closed

A century later the trade route was stopped by the Muslim **TURKS**. But Europeans still wanted a route to China for the spices, silver and gold, one that they could more easily control – this meant finding a sea route.

By the 15th century things were getting worse for the Europeans. Turks now controlled North Africa as well as the **MIDDLE EAST**. They refused to let Christian Europeans go east to China or south across the Sahara Desert.

Europe depended on gold and silver, not paper, to use as money.

By the 15th century most of the European mines were exhausted, so the Europeans had to find some more. One good supply was West Africa, an area that came to be called the Gold Coast. But it was reached by crossing the Sahara Desert. West Africa was also a source of slaves. With that route closed, gold and silver, spices and slaves became more difficult to get.

Henry the Navigator

The first expeditions to try to find a sea route that bypassed the Turks were started in 1420 by Prince Henry of Portugal, known for this as Henry the Navigator (picture ②). He wanted to see if his sailors could go around Africa and get to China by sea. If they could do this, Portugal would not be at the mercy of the Turks.

His sailors went south along the African coast and reached the Gold Coast and so secured their supply of gold. Finally, in 1487 Bartolomeu Dias rounded the Cape of Good Hope at the southern tip of Africa and proved that it was indeed possible to get to the Indian Ocean (picture ①). In 1498 Vasco da Gama sailed all the way to India.

▲ ① Henricus Martellus was a German map maker who created this map in 1489. Compare it to the map of the world on page 5 and you will see that mapmakers now put north at the top. Because of Portuguese exploration there had been a huge increase in the known world in just a few years. But the Portuguese merchants, who paid for the explorations, kept as much information to themselves as possible, so Martellus had to rely on heresay. Notice there is no America.

▶ ② A monument to Henry the Navigator.

The great western adventure

Spanish rulers decided to allow Christopher Columbus to sail west because Portugal already had control of the African coast.

The Spanish soon noticed the success that the Portuguese were having.

Portugal already had forts all along the western coast of Africa, so blocked Spain out of African trade.

In 1492 an Italian captain called Christopher Columbus came to their notice (picture ①). He had been going around the courts of Europe trying to get the money to make an expedition across the Atlantic and find China from the west. Now the Spanish were in a mood to listen.

As a result, the Spanish decided to fund Christopher Columbus' expedition plans. So, as you can see, the decision to go west was made because of a blockage by one country and competition between two others.

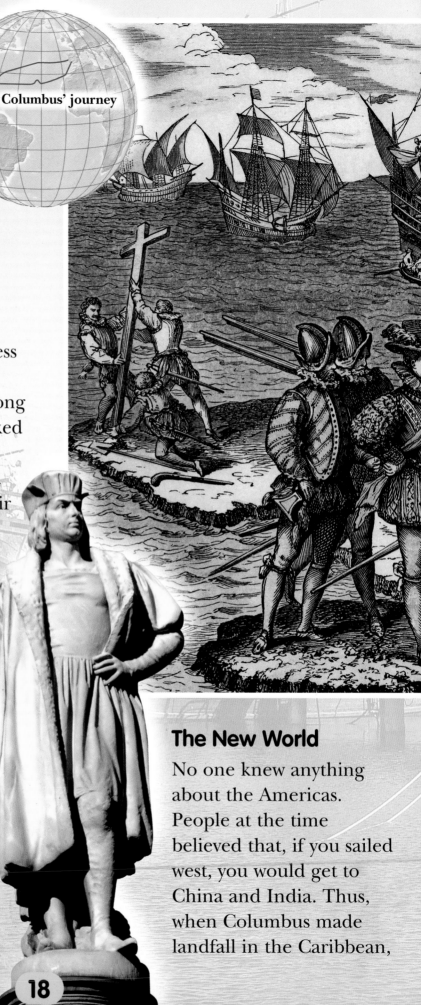

Columbus' journey

▶ ① A statue of Christopher Columbus.

The New World

No one knew anything about the Americas. People at the time believed that, if you sailed west, you would get to China and India. Thus, when Columbus made landfall in the Caribbean,

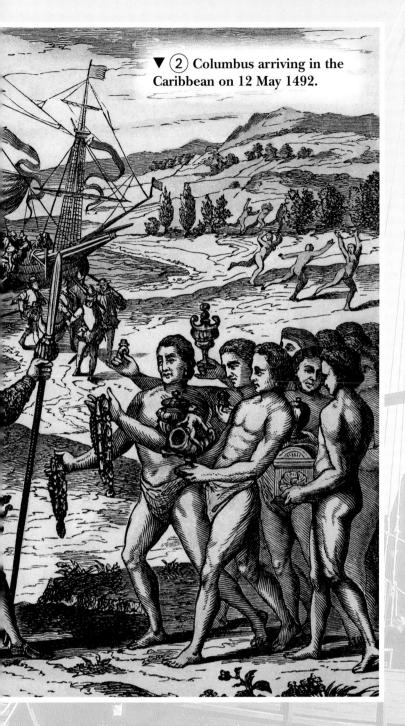

▼ ② Columbus arriving in the Caribbean on 12 May 1492.

Carving up the world

Now Portugal and Spain were competing head on, and they looked to the Pope to help. The Pope declared that everything outside of Europe east of an agreed line was Portuguese (that is, Africa, western Asia and eastern South America (Brazil)), while everything west was to belong to the Spanish.

The result of this single decision cannot be underestimated. It meant that if Spain was to gain more land, it had to claim it from the west.

The Spaniards were not very happy. The Caribbean Islands had no gold or spices. They decided that the only thing to do was to set up colonies, grow things the Spaniards wanted back home and begin a trade route that way. This is why Spain began to colonise the area west of the Caribbean. They later found they had been 'given' a land full of gold by the Pope – Mexico.

The New World was not, however, empty, nor was it 'new' to those who had lived there for tens of thousands of years as the Europeans found. There were empires as large as those in Europe. The conquest of the Aztecs in Mexico is probably the most famous war between a European people and an American people. (You can find out more about this in the *Curriculum Visions Explorers'* book *Exploring the Aztec empire.*)

in 1492, he thought he was in India (and this is why Native Americans were called '**INDIANS**') (picture ②).

Instead of Asia, he had found what came to be called the New World – America. By 1500, the Portuguese navigator, Pedro Álvares Cabral had sailed the same way and also discovered another new world – Brazil.

England's search for wealth

Spain and Portugal had begun to divide up the New World and the FAR EAST between them before England joined in the race. Now it was time for the English to get some of the wealth for themselves.

By the time the first of the Tudors, Henry VII (left), became king, England had to face a world rapidly becoming a **COLONY** of Spain and Portugal. These new colonies promised to make Spain, in particular, even more wealthy and powerful than it already was. This did not please Henry at all.

Since even one small bag of nutmeg could make a person wealthy, Tudor merchants and kings were very interested in having a part of, or better still, in controlling, this New World trade.

Ignoring the Pope

What was Henry to do? There was no hesitation: just like the Dutch and the French, he chose to ignore the decree of the Pope (even though all three countries were Catholic at the time).

Portugal loses out

Portugal was a small country and its forces could not defend its huge empire, so the new exploring nations set up trading posts in the African and Asian lands of Portugal. As a result, some of the wealth that had previously gone to Portugal now started to go to England, the Netherlands and France. Portugal's control of the world grew weaker.

John Cabot

Henry VII wanted the New World, too. To gain these lands he needed captains who would take on a journey into the unknown. He had, however, to avoid lands claimed by the Spanish as Spain was a more powerful country than England.

Just as the Spanish had used Christopher Columbus (an Italian) as captain, so Henry used John Cabot (born in Italy as Giovanni Caboto). Cabot had wanted to work for the Spanish, but they were not interested in him. Henry VII, however, was. So, sometime between 1493 and 1495, Cabot moved with his family to Bristol, the home of many of England's most wealthy merchants. These independently-minded people now had an experienced sailor to send on a new mission.

Fortunately for the English, Spain had ignored North America north of Florida. It was occupied with colonies in Mexico and South America. So the English task (like that of the French) was to search for useful lands to the north.

In 1496, Henry VII granted John Cabot, Cabot's sons, and other Bristol merchants authorisation (known as Letters Patent) to discover, search, and settle lands which were "unknown to Christians". The king wrote that he gave his permission to his:

"well-beloved John Cabot... to seeke out, discover and finde whatsoever isles, countries, regions or provinces... which before this time have been unknown to all Christians."

Cabot eventually set sail in the ship named the Matthew in May 1497 (picture ①). He reached the east coast of North America and named the spot Cape Bonavista (cape of the fine view) – now part of Canada – on 24 June.

▼ ① The departure of John Cabot and his son on their first voyage of discovery, 1497.

Newfoundland

◀ ② John Cabot discovered Newfoundland.

A new island

Cabot had landed on one of the northern capes of Newfoundland (picture ②). He 'took' the area in the name of King Henry VII and called it the "New Found Land". His sailors were able to catch huge numbers of cod simply by dipping baskets into the water. Cabot was rewarded with the sum of £10 by the king for discovering a new island off the coast of what was thought to be China. The king would have been far more generous if Cabot had actually found China or brought home spices.

In 1498, John Cabot was given permission by Henry VII to take ships on a new expedition to continue west from the point he had reached on his first voyage. The aim was to discover Japan. He set out from Bristol with 300 men in May 1498. The five ships carried supplies for a year's travelling. Cabot and his crews were never heard of again. England would have to wait before she could claim a large, useful colony.

In fact it was yet another Italian, Giovanni da Verrazzano, working for the French, who was the first European ever to land in what is now the USA. He reached what is now North Carolina in 1525. He was disappointed to find it did not contain a wealthy people like the Aztecs.

The Northwest Passage

Cabot and Verrazzano were hoping to find a new trading route to Asia around the north of the Americas. It was called the Northwest Passage. But, while they never found such a passage, they did make landfall and set the stage for the English and French colonisation of North America.

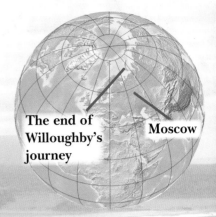

▶ ③ The Northeast Passage: Willoughby's journey ended in tragedy, while Chancellor made it overland from the White Sea to Moscow.

The end of Willoughby's journey

Moscow

The Northeast Passage

Unlike his father, Henry VIII was not all that interested in overseas trade. Then Henry died. His son, Edward VI, was much more interested in trade and he agreed that the Mystery and Company of **MERCHANT ADVENTURERS** for the Discovery of Regions, Dominions, Islands, and Places unknown be established. It was founded in London in about 1551 by Richard Chancellor, Sebastian Cabot and Sir Hugh Willoughby.

In 1553 Sir Hugh Willoughby set out as captain of the Bona Esperanza with two other vessels, one of which was under the command of Richard Chancellor (picture ③). They aimed to find a passage to China by going northeast across the Arctic Ocean.

The vessels were separated by storms as they were crossing the Norwegian Sea. On 14 September Willoughby sailed into a bay near the present border between Finland and Russia. Richard Chancellor reached the White Sea, from where he made his way overland to Moscow to visit Tsar (king) Ivan the Terrible of Russia. This allowed him to set up trade with Russia. Willoughby was not so lucky. His ship with the frozen crew, including Captain Willoughby and his journal, were found by fishermen a year later.

Further English journeys of exploration by merchants led to the creation of the East India Company in 1600, and then the Virginia Company in 1609.

Frobisher and the Inuit

Baffin Island and the Labrador coast

Martin Frobisher was one of the earliest Tudor explorers to seek a Northwest Passage to China.

Martin Frobisher was in search of the Northwest Passage. But his meetings with the Inuit resulted in disaster.

In the summer of 1576 a group of Inuit, the Native Americans who lived on Baffin Island, Canada, were making their way to their summer hunting grounds on the coast.

At the same time, Captain Martin Frobisher and a crew of 35, set sail from London in two small 20 ton ships, the Gabriel and Michael.

During a storm, the Michael was abandoned, so it was only the Gabriel that sighted land on 28 July. They had found Labrador. Then they pressed on and reached Baffin Island on 18 August, 1576.

The first journey

The Inuit and the English were both amazed to see each other. The Inuits were fascinated, got into their kayaks and paddled out to the Gabriel. The Inuits offered trade and also said one of them would show Frobisher farther west. First the Inuit wanted to return to their camp and Frobisher sent some of his men with them. Frobisher told his men not to go out of sight, but for some reason they disobeyed him. Frobisher mistakenly thought his men had been captured. He only had 18 men left, and he did not think he could risk them, so he took an Inuit captive and sailed back to England. The crew on land were now abandoned, although they had not been harmed, and so the first contact in the north began with a misunderstanding. It would not be the last.

Frobisher took back samples of rock, which some people believed was gold. So he was able to get a much bigger expedition together the next year.

A Company of Cathay (Cathay was then the term for China) was established, giving the company the sole right of sailing in every direction but the east.

The second journey

On 17 July, 1577, the expedition of 120 men, including miners, arrived back at Labrador and claimed the land for the queen. The Inuit arrived again (picture ①). Now each side was wary of the other but they still traded. Then, just as the ships were about to leave, there was another misunderstanding, resulting in a fight between the soldiers of the

▼ ① Frobisher meeting the Inuits on his second voyage to Baffin Island in 1577.

One of Frobisher's expedition was the artist John White who drew the first pictures of the Inuit in 1577 and who later went back with Walter Raleigh to draw the native peoples near Roanoke in 1585–6.

expedition and the Inuits. Attempts were also made to recover the men lost the previous year, but with no success. The expedition returned to England with their ore, which proved not to be gold at all. In fact, it was worthless.

The third journey

Despite all these drawbacks, there was more enthusiasm than ever to make discoveries and plans were drawn up to start a mining colony of over 100 men. They arrived back at Labrador in July 1578 and made an attempt at founding a settlement. They also collected more rock, hoping that would be gold, but arguments broke out and the settlement was not established. They left in August. The ore was again worthless and Frobisher made no further journeys.

Elizabeth's pirates

England was not a wealthy country. Elizabeth could not afford to send out explorers in the way the Spanish were doing. But England could attack the loot-bearing ships being brought back by the Spanish. Elizabeth turned an official blind eye.

When King Edward died, his sister Mary became queen. When Queen Mary died Elizabeth became queen (picture ①). By now, the extra wealth Spain was getting from her colonies allowed her to pay for wars against other European countries, including England.

England wanted a share of this wealth. Her involvement with Frobisher (page 24) in founding a colony had not gone well. So a different approach was taken.

Queen Elizabeth gave permission for some of England's best sailors to become **PRIVATEERS**. They would go off, funded by London or Bristol merchants, and take treasure from the Spanish and Portuguese – if they could. The places they attacked the Spanish ships were the areas close to the Caribbean and the Spanish ports. This was called the **SPANISH MAIN**.

▲ ① Queen Elizabeth I.

◀ ② Francis Drake.

▼ ③ Drake captured the Cacafuego on his voyage around the world (see page 30).

Spain started a system of convoys to protect itself from the privateers and there were few successful attacks upon these convoys. More treasure reached Spain in the period 1585–1603 than at any other time in history. Even so, privateers were of great benefit to Elizabeth because they brought much needed gold and silver to England.

Famous privateers

The most famous British privateer was Sir Francis Drake (pictures ② and ③). However, Captain Christopher Newport led more attacks on Spanish shipping and settlements than any other English privateer. During the war with Spain, Newport seized Spanish and Portuguese treasure in fierce sea battles in the West Indies. In 1592, Newport captured the Portuguese ship, Madre de Dios. His men collected 500 tons of spices, silks, gemstones and other treasures. It was the most valuable prize captured during Elizabethan privateering times.

London becomes a centre of trade

At home, the privateers brought a double bonus to Elizabethan England. As well as the booty from their raids, they also helped to turn England – and London in particular – into a centre of trade.

Elizabethan palaces such as Longleat, Wollaton and Hardwick, are among the biggest palaces ever built in England.

Exploration and the Slave Trade

As Portugal and Spain formed colonies, so they spread European diseases to which the native peoples had no immunity. This caused enormous numbers of deaths. The Europeans at first used the native peoples as workers on the sugar and tobacco PLANTATIONS they set up, but as the number of native people got smaller, so they had to look around for others to work on the estates.

One source was from Africa, where Portugal already had trading posts. When African nations fought wars, anyone they captured became a slave. These were offered for sale to the Portuguese. From about 1545 Portugal started shipping slaves to Brazil. Thus the Age of Discovery and the need for labour began the Atlantic SLAVE TRADE. During Tudor times England was not involved in the slave trade, although, when it got its own colonies, it became, like the other colonial powers, very dependent on slaves.

Weblink: www.CurriculumVisions.com

Around the world

In the search for ways of getting to the Far East, explorers, including Ferdinand Magellan and Sir Francis Drake, became the first to sail right around the world.

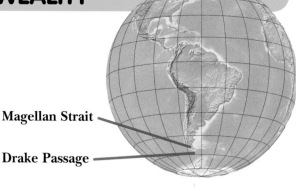

Magellan Strait

Drake Passage

▲ ① Near the bottom of South America Magellan found a strait (Magellan Strait). Thirty eight days later he sailed out into the Pacific Ocean. Francis Drake also sailed through the Magellan Strait. He was then blown off-course and became the first explorer to sail in to the Antarctic Ocean (Drake Passage).

The Pope had declared that Spain could own anything found by travelling west. So, while one of Spain's explorers, Hernan Cortes, was invading the land of the Aztecs in Mexico, Spain was also sending Ferdinand Magellan west in search of the Spice Islands (modern Indonesia). To be successful, Magellan had to travel around the south of South America (picture ①). Although Magellan was later killed in the Philippines, his crew became the first men to sail entirely around the world in a single journey. It took three years.

Around the world with Sir Francis Drake

Sir Francis Drake spent much of his early life as a privateer, but he was an adventurous man, always given to take up a challenge. In 1577, Drake was sent by Queen Elizabeth to claim land along the Pacific coast of North America and so prevent the Spanish from getting it. He set out aboard his flagship, the Pelican, together with the Elizabeth, the Marygold, the Swan and the Benedict (later renamed the Christopher) (picture ③ pages 30–31). In all there were over 160 men.

South America

After crossing the Atlantic, Drake made contact with the Native Americans. At this point he found two ships unseaworthy and he scrapped them. He renamed his flagship the Golden Hind in honour of the hind on the coat of arms of Sir Christopher Hatton (see pages 9–11). The three ships sailed through the Magellan Strait, but were then caught in great storms and blown off-course. The smallest ship (the Marygold) sank and one other (the Elizabeth) turned back to England, so it was only the Golden Hind that eventually sailed north along the Pacific coast of South America, attacking Spanish ports and capturing some Spanish ships and their treasure.

▼ ② Sir Francis Drake (1540–1596) meeting the peoples of Nova Albion. They treated him like a king.

Nova Albion

On 17 June, 1579, Drake landed somewhere north of Spain's northernmost settlement, probably in California (picture ②). He claimed the land for the English Crown and called it Nova Albion, meaning "New Britain". It set England's claim to the entire coast.

Drake then sailed west across the Pacific, and a few months later reached what is modern Indonesia – the Spice Islands. While there, the Golden Hind became caught on a reef and was almost destroyed.

He then went round the Cape of Good Hope in southern Africa, and reached Sierra Leone on 22 July, 1580.

On 26 September the Golden Hind sailed into Plymouth with Drake and 59 remaining crew, along with a rich cargo of spices and captured Spanish treasures. The Queen's half-share of the cargo was worth more than the rest of the crown's income for that entire year. Drake was the first Englishman to sail around the world and he was knighted by Queen Elizabeth aboard the Golden Hind on 4 April, 1581.

The Queen then ordered all written accounts of Drake's voyage to be classed as secret, and its crew were sworn to silence on pain of death. She wanted to keep Drake's success a secret from Spain.

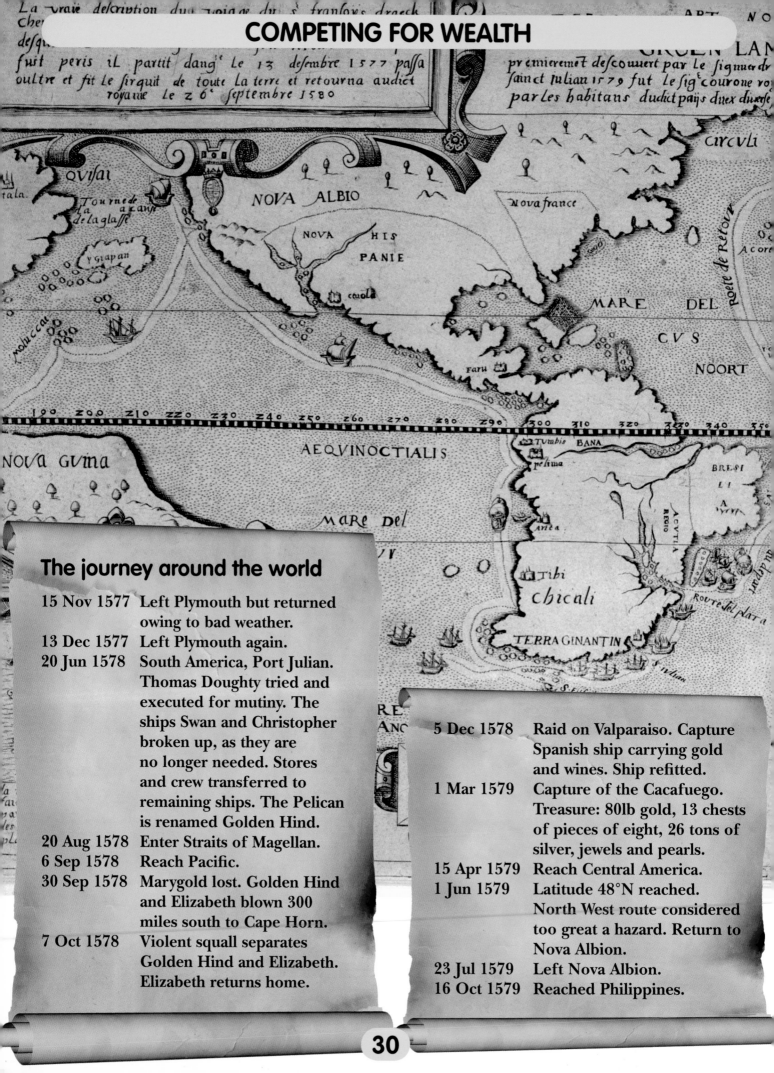

The journey around the world

15 Nov 1577 Left Plymouth but returned owing to bad weather.
13 Dec 1577 Left Plymouth again.
20 Jun 1578 South America, Port Julian. Thomas Doughty tried and executed for mutiny. The ships Swan and Christopher broken up, as they are no longer needed. Stores and crew transferred to remaining ships. The Pelican is renamed Golden Hind.
20 Aug 1578 Enter Straits of Magellan.
6 Sep 1578 Reach Pacific.
30 Sep 1578 Marygold lost. Golden Hind and Elizabeth blown 300 miles south to Cape Horn.
7 Oct 1578 Violent squall separates Golden Hind and Elizabeth. Elizabeth returns home.

5 Dec 1578 Raid on Valparaiso. Capture Spanish ship carrying gold and wines. Ship refitted.
1 Mar 1579 Capture of the Cacafuego. Treasure: 80lb gold, 13 chests of pieces of eight, 26 tons of silver, jewels and pearls.
15 Apr 1579 Reach Central America.
1 Jun 1579 Latitude 48°N reached. North West route considered too great a hazard. Return to Nova Albion.
23 Jul 1579 Left Nova Albion.
16 Oct 1579 Reached Philippines.

▼ ③ Map showing Francis Drake's CIRCUMNAVIGATION of the globe, late 16th century.

3 Nov 1579	Reached Spice Islands (Indonesia). Trade agreement made with Sultan of Ternate. 6 tons of cloves taken aboard.
9 Jan 1580	Ship strikes a reef; 8 cannon and 3 tons of cloves jettisoned. Wind changed and ship slid off reef.
26 Mar 1580	Reached Java and left for Cape of Good Hope.
22 July 1580	Reached Sierra Leone.
26 Sep 1580	Return to Plymouth.

Sir Humphrey Gilbert

Humphrey Gilbert was an adventurer who became the first English property owner in North America. He meant to set up the first English colony, but failed.

Sir Humphrey Gilbert was another adventurer convinced that he could find the Northwest Passage to Cathay.

Gilbert was one of the backers of the failed expeditions by Martin Frobisher (page 24). He then led an expedition of fifteen ships to North America, but none of them made landfall. In 1583 Gilbert set sail with a small fleet of five vessels in June, including one vessel owned and commanded by his half brother Sir Walter Raleigh (pronounced 'Rawley' at that time) (picture ①). The ships eventually arrived at Newfoundland.

By this date fishermen from all parts of Europe had already been using the coast as a summer base, sailing out to it each spring and returning in the autumn. It was a kind of no-man's land, not claimed by any country.

When Gilbert arrived with his authority from the Queen, this changed and the area became a crown colony on 5 August, 1583 (picture ②). This is how Gilbert became the first English property owner in North America. The first thing Gilbert did was to demand tax money from the fishermen!

However, Gilbert did not have enough supplies to start his planned settlement. On the way back his little ship sank and he was drowned.

Although Gilbert had landed with his paper of authority, Newfoundland did not really become a colony until 1610. But what was most important was that the right to explore (called Letters Patent) were transferred to Walter Raleigh in 1584, who then made the first determined effort to start a colony. That was at Roanoke.

▶ ① Walter Raleigh.

▲ ② St John's is the oldest English-founded settlement in North America. The city earned its name when explorer John Cabot became the first European to sail into the harbour, on 24 June, 1497 – the feast day of Saint John the Baptist. Within a few years the harbour became known to European fishermen and by 1540 French, Spanish and Portuguese crossed the Atlantic annually to fish the waters.

In about 1546 Water Street was first laid out, making it the oldest street in North America.

On 5 August, 1583, Sir Humphrey Gilbert claimed the area as England's first overseas colony under Royal Charter of Queen Elizabeth I. At the time, he found 16 English ships and 20 French and Portuguese vessels using the harbour, so it was hardly a ground-breaking exploration.

The first permanent settlers arrived at St John's in 1605. By 1620 the fishermen of England's West Country had excluded other nations from most of the east coast.

The first English settlement in the New World: Roanoke

The first English settlement in the New World was founded as a result of the ambitions of Sir Walter Raleigh.

▲ ① **The Native American village of Secotan – about 1585. It shows dancing, cooking, the longhouses and corn crops being grown.**

At first, Queen Elizabeth I was not keen on the idea of setting up a colony.

In 1583, the Queen forbade Raleigh to go on what turned out to be the ill-fated voyage he had sponsored with Gilbert. Nevertheless, Raleigh continued to organise and pay for exploration in North America with the aim of finding and mining gold and increasing trade.

Exploration

Queen Elizabeth wanted a base from which to send her privateers on raids against the treasure fleets of Spain.

In 1584, Raleigh paid for an expedition of two small boats to America. It was led by Philip Amadas and Arthur Barlowe. They chose the Outer Banks of modern North Carolina (picture ②).

The chosen site happened to be land owned by the Native Secotan Americans (picture ①). The Europeans were met by Grananimeo, the head of the Secotans in nearby Roanoke Island.

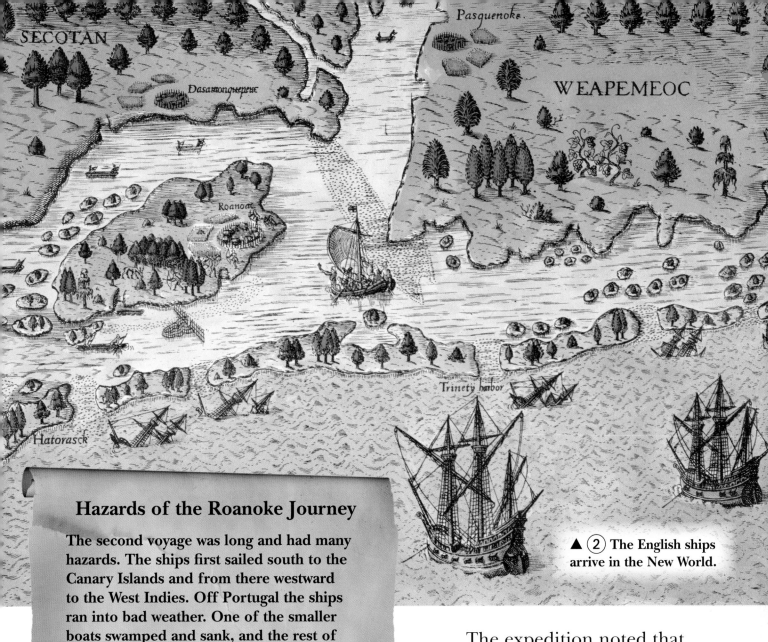

SECOTAN

Pasquenoke.

Dasamonquepeuc

WEAPEMEOC

Roanoac

Trinety harbor

Hatorasck

▲ ② The English ships arrive in the New World.

Hazards of the Roanoke Journey

The second voyage was long and had many hazards. The ships first sailed south to the Canary Islands and from there westward to the West Indies. Off Portugal the ships ran into bad weather. One of the smaller boats swamped and sank, and the rest of the fleet was scattered. Alone, the Tyger sailed on to the proposed rendezvous point near Puerto Rico, then a possession of Spain. There the English built a temporary fort for protection while they built a new ship. A week later they were alarmed to see masts on the horizon. They were relieved when the Elizabeth, separated from them a month earlier and 3,000 miles away, came into sight. With delays caused by the capture of a Spanish ship, the need to gather salt, and the purchase of supplies, the English finally reached the Outer Banks on the 26th of June. On the 29th of June 1585 the Tyger ran aground at Wococon and lost most of its supplies.

The expedition noted that they were "*very handsome and goodly people, and in their behaviour as mannerly, and civil as any of Europe*" – pictures ④ (page 37) and ⑤ (page 39). The Native Americans and the expedition traded: leather, coral, dyes and much more in exchange for hatchets, axes and knives. Grananimeo also provided the Europeans with a large amount of food provisions. In September, two Native Americans – Manteo and Wanchese – agreed to go back to England with the expedition.

▲ ③ What the colony at Roanoke might have looked like.

The arrival of trade goods and the Native Americans, together with stories of the bountifulness of the country, made people in England even more enthusiastic about settling. Raleigh named the place the expedition had visited Virginia, in honour of the Virgin Queen.

Roanoke

In 1585, Raleigh organised a voyage to take 300 colonists to Roanoke Island in seven ships. It included a detachment of troops led by Ralph Lane, who was also a fortifications expert. Sir Richard Grenville led the expedition.

The settlers were well received by the Native Americans, and they allowed the English to build a fort and some cottages (picture ③).

However, over the coming months, relations became strained as the English wanted more and more food. This put pressure on the food supplies of the Native Americans.

At the same time, a curious thing happened. Wherever the English had been, many people started to die. Just as was happening to the Aztecs in the south, the English were bringing diseases for which the Native Americans had no immunity.

Meanwhile, relations with the local Native Americans continued to sour and food supplies for everyone were low. Chief Wingina did not have enough reserves for his own people and certainly not enough to feed more than 100 Englishmen.

▼ ④ 'The Manner of their Fishing', c1585–c1593. John White composed or 'invented' this scene by basing it on several studies, combining three methods of fishing used by the Native Algonquian Americans. By day, they used a dip net and spear, and by night, a fire in a canoe to attract the fish to the boat.

Weblink: www.CurriculumVisions.com

And then Ensinore, the last influential friend of the English, died. Having learned of a plot to attack the English, Lane struck first and burned the Native American village of Dasamonquepeuc. With the words "Christ our Victory" as the signal, Lane and his men, who had entered the village under the pretence of discussing a complaint, attacked the Native Americans and beheaded the chief.

Without the goodwill of the Native Americans, the colonists now had a very hard time finding enough food, since they were not familiar with the plants and animals around them.

Added to this, the colony's relief fleet had not even left England by Easter, the date Lane expected it to arrive in America. In June 1586, Sir Francis Drake, fresh from attacking Spanish bases in the West Indies and Florida, made a planned stopover at Roanoke Island. He offered Lane one month's supplies and a ship that could carry them all back to England. This first settlement had failed.

The last chance

The next year Raleigh sent a new expedition under John White (who was also an artist and who had been with Frobisher on the second Baffin Island expedition). It had 150 settlers on board. They reoccupied the Roanoke village. There John White's daughter gave birth to the first English child to be born in North America. But now it was too late to plant crops and John White feared the Native Americans would not trade with him, so he set off to England, planning a quick return trip. However, once in England all ships were needed as protection against the threat of a Spanish invasion (the Armada).

◀ ⑤ Native American village of Pomeiock, Gibbs Creek, North Carolina, 1585, showing huts and longhouses inside a protective palisade. Sketch by John White.

by the lack of supplies and local knowledge. Although prepared to farm, they lacked the supplies and knowledge of local crops. They were also hampered by the ill-will of the Native Americans, which had been caused by the first colonists.

The affect of the colonists on the Native Americans

These first meetings between the English colonists and the Native Americans had mixed results. While some of the colonists and Native Americans seemed to have got along for a time, the heavy-handed way the colonists treated the Native Americans made them many enemies. The English would have felt themselves superior to the natives and, since the natives were not Christians, would have felt justified in treating them badly. These encounters almost certainly taught the Native Americans that they would need to be very careful in their dealings with any future colonists.

From trade, England learned of some foods and other products for the first time. Walter Raleigh is given the credit for introducing both tobacco and potatoes to Britain, although both of these were already known from Spanish explorers.

In fact it took three years before White was able to get enough backing for the return journey. When he got there the settlement was empty. No one knows what happened to all the settlers he left behind.

What went wrong?

The second group of colonists were better prepared for their settlement than the first but they were hampered

▼ ① This is what the first Jamestown fort may have looked like.

The first proper colony: Jamestown

Just three years after Elizabeth dies, the colony at Jamestown becomes the first permanent English settlement in what is now the United States.

In June 1606, King James I, who had become king after the death of Elizabeth, allowed a group of London merchants, called the Virginia Company, to start a trading post in North America.

Three ships left Plymouth with 108 men and boys, and instructions to settle Virginia, find gold and a sea route to China. There were no women on these first ships. It took 144 days, and 40 people died at sea.

They made landfall on 26 April, 1607, and named the site Cape Henry, in honour of Henry Frederick, Prince of Wales, the eldest son of King James. Sealed orders from the Virginia Company were opened which told them to seek an inland site for their settlement which would give protection from enemy (Spanish) ships.

Jamestown is founded

In the following days, the ships sailed inland upstream along the James River (naming it after the king) looking for a suitable location for their settlement. On 14 May, 1607, the colonists chose Jamestown Island partly because it was not occupied by Native Americans.

The first fort

The settlers quickly set about building a fort (pictures ① and ②). Within a month, James Fort covered an acre on Jamestown Island. However, it soon became apparent why the Native Americans did not live there. Jamestown Island was a swamp and away from most areas suited to hunting game such as deer and bears. It was also infested with mosquitoes and the salty water of the tidal James River was not good to drink.

Trouble sets in

Many of the settlers were not well-equipped for such a hard life. Some were 'gentlemen' not accustomed to manual or skilled labour; the others were farmers. They were short of skilled craftsmen. Many suffered from saltwater poisoning and most of the early settlers died of disease and starvation.

For the first two years the colony survived on supplies brought from England. Despite these troubles, more settlers arrived. By the time the investors in London sent out their second supply ship, having received no gold or anything else valuable from the colonists, their patience was starting to run out. They demanded that the colonists start paying their way. The new governor of the colony, John Smith, talked the investors around, convincing them that profits would come eventually.

▼ ② One of the houses in the reconstructed James Fort at Jamestown, USA.

Smith was a good leader and he managed to set up some trade with the local Native Americans. But relations with them were never good. Smith was attacked by the local Powhatan Americans during a trip upriver and (legend has it) was only saved by the pleas of Chief Powhatan's young daughter, Pocahontas (picture ③).

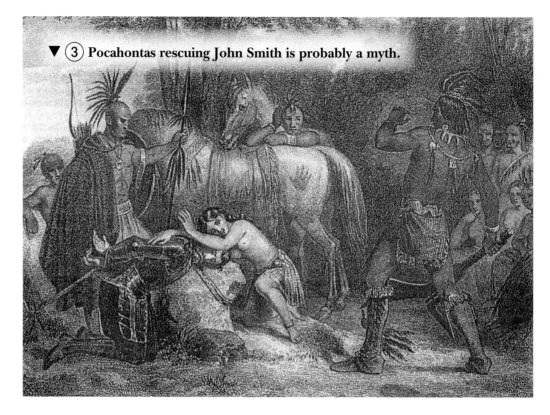

▼ ③ Pocahontas rescuing John Smith is probably a myth.

Edge of starvation

The colonists had not planned to grow their own food. Instead, they expected that trade with the locals would supply them with enough food between supply ships. But the Native Americans had very little spare food to start with. The Jamestown colonists could not have known it, but they had arrived during a bad drought.

The winter of 1609–1610 became known as the "starving time" as over 80 per cent of the 500 settlers died of starvation. It took a new governor, Lord de la Ware, and his supply ships to get the colony back on its feet.

John Rolfe

John Rolfe was the first man successfully to grow and export tobacco in the colony. Rolfe was able to make his fortune. It was he who married the Native American Princess Pocahontas on 24 April, 1614.

Once tobacco had been established as an export cash crop, investors became more interested and groups of them united to create **PLANTATIONS** called 'hundreds'.

By 1617, the colonists were exporting 50,000 pounds of tobacco a year to England and were beginning to make enough money to make sure they could survive and prosper. Meanwhile the Native Americans were beginning to realise that the colonists were here to stay.

Plymouth Colony

The Plymouth Colony was founded by a group of people whose religious views made their lives uncomfortable in England. They came to be called the Pilgrims.

The Plymouth Colony was, like Jamestown, a struggle to make succeed. The Pilgrims set sail on the Mayflower, which left Plymouth, England, in September 1620. When they arrived (at a place named Provincetown, near modern Boston, USA) two months later, they were too late to plant crops.

Their leader led an expedition for food, during which they robbed a Native American corn store. However, feeling they had upset the Native Americans, they then moved on and in December founded the town of Plymouth.

All this time they were relying on stores they had brought with them. Then on 16 March, 1621, a Native American named Samoset, walked boldly into the midst of the settlement and proclaimed, "Welcome, Englishmen!". He had learned some English from fishermen who worked off the coast.

The Pilgrims realised they needed the help of the Native Americans and they made a treaty with them. They then stuck by it. This is what made the colony a success.

After terrible years when they nearly starved, the colonists were able to grow enough crops to feed themselves. At the end of the harvest, they thanked God for this. This event was what started the modern holiday of Thanksgiving, one of the most important days in the United States.

▲▼ (4) A reconstruction of the Plymouth colony.

43

What effect has Tudor exploration had on our lives today?

The Age of Discovery opened up new links across the world and began a period of colonisation that lasted for centuries.

The Tudor explorers increased our knowledge of the world – they found new routes to America and Asia that allowed trade. In Asia and Africa, new areas were opened up to European settlement. The explorers brought new spices and goods to Europe.

▲ (1) Potatoes and tomatoes both came from the New World.

Colonisation

The explorers found new lands that had been unknown to Europe, but they took many of those lands from the people who had been living on them. In the Americas, the European explorers conquered local peoples, took away their land and enslaved them. In Asia, the Tudor age explorers traded with the local kings and chieftains, but after Tudor times they would eventually make these lands colonies of England.

Diseases

Explorers from Europe also brought diseases, such as smallpox, that eventually killed millions in the 'New World'.

By colonising America, they began the long history of conflict with the Native Americans, which would end with the death of 90 per cent of these peoples over the next 200 years. The Native American empires in South America were also ended, as European explorers plundered them for gold and gems.

Slave trade

The Tudor explorers were some of the first to begin the slave trade. The slave trade caused much misery and resulted in the forced movement of people from one continent to another.

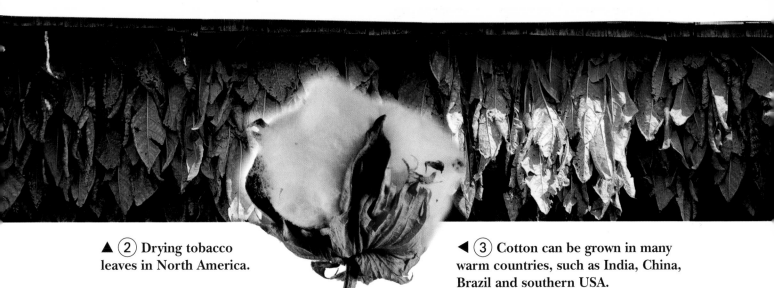

▲ ② Drying tobacco leaves in North America.

◄ ③ Cotton can be grown in many warm countries, such as India, China, Brazil and southern USA.

Wealth

The wealth from the lands the explorers reached would make some European countries wealthy. With the money, new public buildings would be built, artists would flourish, and most people would find that life got better. Styles of cooking changed as spices became more readily available. Cocoa, potatoes, sweet potatoes, tomatoes, squash and corn all came from the new lands in the Americas (picture ①).

Cheaper goods

Crops such as cotton (picture ③) and tobacco (picture ②) could be grown cheaply in the newly colonised areas (using slave labour) so that more people could afford the luxuries of new clothes; and smoking became popular.

Adding to maps and knowledge

The explorers also filled in the map of the world and opened the way for scientists to explore new lands and discover new things.

All of this new knowledge made people more curious about the world around them and eventually changed the way that people thought of the world. Before too long, people no longer thought only of their home town, but began to realise that there was a wider world, and they became interested in it and in learning about it.

The age of exploration is generally said to have ended in the early seventeenth century. By this time European vessels were built well enough and their navigators were competent enough to travel to virtually anywhere they wanted. Exploration, of course, continued. The Arctic and Antarctic seas were not explored until the nineteenth century. It also took much longer for Europeans to explore the interiors of continents, though Spanish conquistadors had already crossed the Amazon Basin and had reached the centre of what is now the United States before the middle of the 16th century.

Weblink: www.CurriculumVisions.com

Glossary

AGE OF DISCOVERY The time, starting in Portugal in the 1420s and ending about 200 years later, in which Europeans looking for gold, silver and spices, visited lands for the first time. The most important results of this were the Europeans forming colonies in America at the expense of the Native American nations.

BALLAST Heavy materials put in the bottom of a ship to help make the ship float upright, just as we might add lead weights to a fishing float. Without this, the heavy masts sticking high above the water would make the ship top-heavy and liable to capsize.

BOWSPRIT A pole extending forward from a sailing vessel's prow. It provides an anchor point for the foremost sail, and an extension to the deck.

CARAVEL A small sailing vessel developed in the 15th century. It was able to get into small waterways and explore inland in places the larger carrack could not reach.

CARRACK The main vessel used in exploring during the Age of Discovery. In a small exploring fleet there would be one carrack supported by two or more caravels. Large carracks were mounted with guns and called galleons.

CIRCUMNAVIGATION To go right round (the world). This never happened in one single journey, but over years, the sailors stopping off in many places during the voyage. When you think how small the vessels were, it is remarkable they succeeded.

CRUSADES The time, about four hundred years before the Age of Discovery, when there were attempts by the Christians of western Europe to take back the city of Jerusalem from the Muslim Turks. They did this because they feared their holy sites were being destroyed. It was a case of mistaken intentions on both sides, but it resulted in conflict that has, in the eyes of some extreme people, lasted through to the present day.

COLONY A country that does not govern itself, but belongs to another country.

DHOW A small sailing vessel designed in Egypt and other Middle Eastern countries. It had a single triangular sail and was good at manoeuvring in shallow river waters.

FAR EAST The lands of Asia east of India. The largest far eastern country was, and still is, China.

FORECASTLE The raised front part of a ship. It was meant to be a place from which marines could fire down on attackers, just as soldiers would have fired down from the battlements of a castle on land.

INDIANS An unfortunate and wholly erroneous term given by Europeans to Native American nations. It came about because the European explorers were looking for India and China on their way west. When they arrived in the Americas they thought they had arrived in India, so they called the people Indians.

MAN O'WAR A carrack that was meant to be a fighting vessel.

MERCHANT A person who buys and sells goods to other traders. He is a wholesaler, buying in bulk and then selling in smaller amounts to those people who finally sell to customers.

MERCHANT ADVENTURER One of a group of people who invested money to fit out a ship with stores and crew. The crew then went off in search of goods from distant lands. It was a risky business, which is why these merchant adventurers were not ordinary merchants. They could lose everything if the ship was lost, but they could also make a fortune if the ship returned with a cargo of spices, silk, gold and other goods.

MIDDLE EAST The lands around the eastern and south-eastern end of the Mediterranean Sea, to the east of Greece and to the west of India. It also includes the coastal areas of eastern North Africa.

PLANTATION A very large farm growing just one type of crop. Plantations in the Age of Discovery were producing tobacco in Virginia.

PRIVATEER A person who set out to rob other people on behalf of his government. He was effectively an official pirate. Privateering came about because countries like England wanted a share of the wealth that Spain and Portugal had gained by colonising America and other places.

SLAVE TRADE The buying and selling of people. Trading in slaves is something that has been going on since earliest times and still goes on today. In Tudor times, it was a perfectly normal way of getting extra labour. Slaves were often people captured in battle. Most Native American nations took slaves, for example, as did most African nations. In the Age of Discovery, Africans were pleased to get rid of those they had beaten in battle because then they would cause them no further problem. The Europeans needed slaves to work plantations as diseases had killed off many Native Americans.

SPANISH MAIN The part of the sea off the coast of Spanish colonies. It was the place where the Spanish treasure fleets departed with gold, silver and other precious cargoes en route to Spain.

STERNCASTLE The defensive castle at the back end of a ship (see forecastle).

TURKS A historic term referring to Muslim peoples, the most powerful of whom were based in Turkey. It corresponded to the Ottoman Empire, ruled from Constantinople (now called Istanbul).

Age of Discovery timeline

1420 Prince Henry the Navigator sends ships along the African coast. He is looking for a way of reaching China.

1487 Bartolomeu Dias rounds the Cape of Good Hope and thus opens the route to India.

1492 Christopher Columbus sets out for China and accidentally reaches the Americas, now called the New World. He calls the people he meets 'Indians' because he thinks he is in India.

1497 John Cabot sets sail to find a Northwest Passage around the top of the Americas and lands in Newfoundland.

1498 Vasco da Gama reaches India.

1500 Pedro Alvares Cabral reaches Brazil.

1525 Giovanni da Verrazzano reaches what is now the United States.

1553 Sir Hugh Willoughby sets sail for a Northeast Passage around Asia and freezes to death in the process.

1562 Jean Ribault starts a Huguenot colony (called Charles Fort) at Port Royal in South Carolina.

   John Hawkins makes his first voyage to the West Indies.

1563 Charles Fort abandoned.

1564 Second colony of Huguenots under Rene de Laudonniere arrives on St John's River in Florida. John Hawkins' second voyage to the West Indies and Guinea.

1567 John Hawkins departs on third voyage.

1576
–1578 Martin Frobisher makes three voyages and meets Inuit in Canada.

1577 Sir Francis Drake leaves for a round the world voyage of discovery.

1578 Humphrey Gilbert sailed for America with 350 men but was forced to return.

1580 Sir Francis Drake returns to England from his voyage around the world.

1583 Sir Humphrey Gilbert's voyage to Newfoundland. His ship was lost on the return voyage.

1584 Philip Amadas and Arthur Barlowe reach Roanoke Island in July, and return to England in September.

1585 Raleigh's fleet of seven vessels under Ralph Lane, reach Roanoke Island in June.

1586 In June, Sir Francis Drake arrives from Florida and removes the Lane colony to England.

1587 John White with 150 men, women and children sent by Sir Walter Raleigh to plant the Cittie of Raleigh on the Chesapeake Bay, landed at Hatorask on 22 July.

1590 John White returns to Roanoke Island.

1602 Nova Scotia visited regularly by English traders.

1603 Captain Martin Pring sent to New England coast by Bristol merchants.

   Captain Bartholomew Gilbert sent on voyage to Chesapeake Bay. Gilbert and four others went ashore (likely the Eastern Shore) and were killed by Native Americans.

1607 Jamestown is founded.

1620 Plymouth Colony is founded.

Index

Africa 4, 16–17, 18, 19, 27, 44
Age of Discovery 4
    and throughout
Age of Discovery (definition) 46
Amadas, Philip 34, 47
astrolabe 13
Aztecs 19, 22, 28, 36

Baffin Island 24, 25
ballast 9, 46
Barlowe, Arthur 34, 47
bowsprit 9, 46
Brazil 19, 27, 47

Cabot, John 20–23, 33, 47
Cabot, Sebastian 23
Cacafuego 27, 30
Canada 21–22, 24–25
Cape of Good Hope 17, 29,
    31, 47
caravel 6, 8, 46
Caribbean 18–19, 26–27
carrack 6, 7, 8, 46
Cathay 24, 32 see also China
Chancellor, Richard 23
Charles Fort 47
China 16, 17, 18, 22, 23, 24,
    40, 47
circumnavigation 28–31, 46
colony 19, 20, 25, 27, 32–43, 44,
    46, 47
Columbus, Christopher 7, 8,
    18–19, 47
Cortes, Hernan 28
cotton 45
Crusades 4, 46

dhow 6, 46
Dias, Bartolomeu 17, 47
diseases 15, 27, 36, 44
Drake, Sir Francis 9–11, 26, 27,
    28–31, 38, 47

East India Company 23
Edward VI 23
Elizabeth I 11, 26–27, 28, 29,
    33, 34

Far East 20, 28, 46
forecastle 7, 8, 46
Frobisher, Martin 24–25, 32, 47

galleon 6, 8, 46
Gama, Vasca da 17, 47
Gilbert, Bartholomew 47
Gilbert, Sir Humphrey
    32–33, 47
gold 4, 16, 17, 19, 24–25, 27, 30,
    34, 40, 44
Golden Hind 9–11, 28–31
Grenville, Sir Richard 36

Hawkins, John 47
Henry the Navigator 17, 47
Henry Tudor (Henry VII)
    20–22
Henry VIII 8, 23
Huguenots 47

Indians – see Native Americans
Inuit 24–25, 47

James I 40
Jamestown 3, 40–42, 47

Labrador 24, 25
Lane, Ralph 36, 38, 47

Magellan Strait 28, 30
Magellan, Ferdinand 28
man o'war 9, 46
Mappa Mundi 5
Martellus 17
merchant 4, 17, 20, 21, 23, 26,
    40, 46
merchant adventurer 23, 46
merchant ship 7, 8
Middle East 16, 46

Native Americans (Indians)
    19, 24–25, 28, 29, 34–43, 44
navigation 6, 12–13
New World (Americas) 8, 18–19,
    20, 30, 32–43, 44–45, 47
Newfoundland 22, 32–33, 47
North Carolina 22, 34, 39
Northeast Passage 23, 47
Northwest Passage 23, 24, 32, 47
Nova Albion 29, 30

ocean hazards 4

Pilgrims 43
pirate 26–27

plantation 27, 42, 46
Plymouth 28–29, 40, 42
Plymouth Colony 43, 47
Pocahontas 42
Polo, Maffeo 16
Polo, Marco 4
Polo, Niccolo 16
Portugal, Portuguese 6, 17, 18,
    19, 20, 26–27
potato 39, 44, 45
Pring, Martin 47
privateer 12, 26–27, 28, 34, 46

quadrant 13

Raleigh, Sir Walter 32,
    34–39, 47
Ribault, Jean 47
Roanoke 32, 34–39, 47
Rolfe, John 42
Russia 23

sailors' illnesses 15
sailors' living conditions 9–15
ship's log 13
ships 6–15
silk 27
silver 4, 16, 17, 19, 27, 30
slave trade 4, 17, 27, 44, 46–47
Smith, John 41, 42
South America 19, 21, 28, 44
Spain, Spanish 18, 19, 20, 26–27,
    28, 38, 45
Spanish Main 26, 47
Spice Islands 28, 29, 31
spices 4, 11, 16, 17, 27, 44, 45, 46
St John's 33
sterncastle 7, 8, 14, 47

tobacco 27, 39, 42, 45
tomato 44, 45
Turks 16, 17, 47

Verrazzano, Giovanni da 22,
    23, 47
Viking explorers 6
Virginia Company 23, 40
Virginia 36, 40

White, John 25, 37, 38–39, 47
Willoughby, Sir Hugh 23, 47
world voyages 28–31